As believers, as a part of our citizenship in the Kingdom of God, it is important for us to not only know why we are here, and who we are to reach, but it also imperative that we know our lines. When we know our lines as believes, we will be able to activate and demonstrate our faith and trust in God, who is the One, who will keep us from falling.

When you saw the title of this book, I can guess what came to mind for you. Nine times out of ten, you most likely thought about a play, a tv show, or a movie, in which all of these categories involved someone "knowing their lines;" in order for their character or their scene to come to life. And in order for it to be successful, they had to do their part. On the other hand, if you were to show up and not have your lines rehearsed and ready, not only would you be unprepared, but you would cause all of the other parts to be stagnant or unfulfilled. The same is true for believers in the Body of Christ. For example, God has the lead role. As the director, creator, and producer of life and creation, God created the world and all words, because the bible says in John 1:1, that in the beginning was the word, and the word was with God, and the word was God. So, he is the Mastermind behind it all. And because He is who He is, the very word that He has given us to speak when we encounter or experience certain things in our lives, (unless we say the lines that He gave us to speak), He cannot move. In short, he is unable to perform the next act. And I don't know about you, but I want to see God move on my behalf when I recite my lines to Him. I want to hear Him say, "Ok I will take it from here", because I have prompted Him to respond and I knew my lines on cue. How about you? Are you ready to see God respond and restore you back

Know Your LINES

The Kingdom Edition

Jenille Baskin

GODZCHILD PUBLICATIONS

Published by Godzchild Publications
a division of Godzchild, Inc.
22 Halleck St., Newark, NJ 07104
www.godzchildproductions.net

Printed in the United States of America 2019 - 1st Edition

Library of Congress Cataloging-in-Publications Data
Know Your Lines/Tenille Baskin

ISBN-13 978-1942705604

1. Baskin Tenille 2.

2019

TABLE OF
Contents

into your rightful place and position seated at His right hand, in that elevated place?

If you answered yes, then I am so glad you have joined me! I hope that as you read and confess your lines, that they will become the language that comes to you like second nature. English or Spanish or other languages may be your first language in the earth realm, but the word of truth is your first language in the spirit, and whether you have fully embraced it or not, we are spirit, we live in a body, and we possess a soul.

Now let's explore our lines together, and I choose to believe a generation of Kingdom citizens who are Strong and Courageous, Bold and Brave, will arise, and turn this world into a better place, and make the name of Jesus Great Again!

Let's Arise and Shine!

Know Your Lines of Praise
& Rejoicing

These lines are for those days that seem as if you are not winning. Maybe you woke up on the wrong side of the bed Maybe you are feeling defeated, or you just feel like there has to be more to life than this. In addition, God gave us our Praise language, as an expression of thanksgiving and gratitude towards Him. I don't think it is by happenstance that the book of Psalms is the longest book in the bible. It should be our everyday language. Your lines of praise not only say "I trust and acknowledge you as my Father and Lord", and yes I still have the victory in spite of , but it also says, I have the power to overcome how I feel, or I will identify whatever seems to be keeping me in a bound or unsettled place, and overcome with my words of praise. Here is the good news about knowing these lines. Every time you recite them, you remind yourself that

He is with you and for you through it all! Every time you claim them, He becomes strength to your weakness. Every time you are down, when you recite these lines, he will bring you up. He will take you to a mountain of praise to minister to the valley of sadness or sickness. These lines will give you the strength to keep on pressing, and moving, and encouraging others even when you feel discouraged yourself.

THESE ARE YOUR LINES:

I will bless the Lord <u>at all times (in every moment, through every situation)</u> and HIS praise will continually be in my mouth!

I will lift my praise above everything to you, my God and my King, and my praise will never cease, for you deserve endless praise!

Your greatness knows no limits and recognizes no boundaries, and no one can comprehend your magnificence!

Father, I pay tribute to you with all my heart, and I give thanks to You! I will tell others about your amazing works, that you would be lifted up above the heavens, until the whole earth knows your glory!

I reverence you Oh Lord, because of who you are! You are wonderful, and your word says that for those who reverence and worship you in spirit and in truth, that they will possess everything important to their life.

So, I thank you Lord and I worship you, because you know what is important in order for me to live my best life!

Oh taste and see, and yes you are Good! I acknowledge you and put my trust in you, and I thank you that when I do, I am blessed and comforted, and my path is directed by You, Most Holy and Faithful God!

Your loving kindness is better than life! Your Joy is Unspeakable, and Your Mercy is Everlasting! Your Majesty and glorious splendor have captivated me!

There is nothing greater than, or mightier than your awesome works! I will and I choose to Rejoice in the Lord Always! Now to Him, the Great I Am, who is able to do exceedingly and abundantly above all I can ask or think, I honor you, I give you praise, and give you glory!

Scripture References: PSALM CHAPTERS 9:1, 33, 34: 1-3, 108:5, 145, EPHESIANS 3:20, PHILIPPIANS 4:4

Know Your Lines When you Need Strength

Some days are harder than others. Whether you are a student in school, or a parent at home. Students have rough days when they are preparing for a test and it seems that nothing they prepared for, was on the exam. Parents have rough days because they want their child to excel in every area and sometimes, the child works at a different pace than the parent desires. But if you are not a student or a parent, then I know you can understand the hard days of work. Working can be the greatest place of joy, or the greatest place of stress. I know sometimes on our jobs, and just with the day to day grind, we could use a little extra help. The boss may be making demands. The spouse may be arguing endlessly. And on top of that, inwardly, there are times when we just can't take it anymore. We shut down. We walk away. We try to get to that safe place, but it seems like God is nowhere to be found. But here is the Good news: God has promised you that He would always be with you, and one thing we know, is that with Him, a promise made, is a promise kept. In order words, when God says it, he will do it. He is not unrighteous to forget your work and labor, and he is not a man that he should lie. God is a promise keeper, and he specializes in keeping his word. So these lines are words and reminders that you can keep with you, when those days are hectic, when the kids need this, and when your husband/ or significant other is asking you to do this; when the church ministry needs that, or when your work day has just been long, but you know you need to finish strong. When you find yourself needing strength, think of these things:

THESE ARE YOUR LINES:

Father, I thank you that you are my strength, my source of courage, and my strong tower!

You are my invincible army and my shield in whom I take refuge. With you I am strong and safe.

You said, "let the weak SAY that I am strong", and even though I may not feel like it, or even when I may feel a little overwhelmed, I believe in the power of what I say!

So right now, I believe that I am increased in my strength, renewed in my mind, and refreshed in my spirit.

Father, you also said that "your strength is made perfect in my weakness", which means that in those times where I feel like I cannot find the words to say, you will make your way to come and see about me and allow your strength to override my lack.

Thank you for being my very present help.

Thank you for showing me that you are there for me and that you care for me.

Thank you that I can move forward and go on about my day, knowing that you are 100% behind me, you are my invincible army, and I know that I can do all things through Christ, which strengthens me.

Now unto Him who is able to do exceedingly and abundantly above all I can ask or think, thank you, and it is done!

Scripture References: PSALMS CHAPTERS 28:7, 46:1, ISAIAH 40:31, II CORINTHIANS 12:9, JEREMIAH 16:19, EPHESIANS 3:20, PHILIPPIANS 4: 13

Know Your Lines In Order to Conquer Negativity/Naysayers

In my latter years of life experiences, I have come to find that Negativity and Naysayers are neighbors. They have similar purposes and goals. Simply put, they are consumers of time and energy, and they come to merely distract you and take you into a wavering place. I follow and honor Bishop TD Jakes, and one of the things that he said (which has helped me tremendously in my thinking when it comes to Negativity and Naysayers) is this: "What others have to say about me, is none of my business." In other words, I cannot justify the time wasted on why someone does not like me, or how someone prejudged me before they got to know me. This is wasted time, and our time is valuable, so therefore, I have learned my lesson. Now, I immediately close the door to negativity and naysayers. And instead, I invite "God's lines" in. There is a saying that says, "when you know better, you do better". And now that you know, I think when you confront these neighbors immediately, with your lines, these two neighbors (Negativity and Naysayers) will no longer ruin your entire day or take up so much time and space in your head. Never allow anything to cause you to lose track of your purpose. Never let anything or anyone cause you to forget who and whose you are! No, instead of giving room to that enemy of distraction, we have committed to speak our lines, so that we remain in an elevated place. That place and positioning that is so rightfully ours, which is seated in heavenly places, at the right hand of our Father, who Reigns, who goes to bat for us, who will make our enemies our footstool, and who loves us more than anything and anyone. Now to Him who is able to do exceedingly and abundantly above all I can ask or think, thank you, and it is so done.

THESE ARE YOUR LINES:

Father I thank you that you created me in your image, and I thank you that I have the mind of Christ.

In times when I must face negative people or situations, or naysayers that try and control and consume me, I thank you that Greater is He that is in me, than he that is in the world.

Therefore, I have the power to cut the ties and the thoughts, and recenter my thoughts on what you said.

Your word tells me to continually center my mind and concentrate my heart on things that are true, honorable, worthy of respect, right and confirmed by Your word.

So I will focus on things that will bring peace, so that I can remain in my rightful place, which is above, and never beneath.

I no longer make myself at home in the thoughts, actions, and pre-judgements of other people and things that are contradictory to what you said about me.

I am your workmanship, and I am a work of art.

You created me to do good works, and you promised that what you started in me, you would perfect and complete until the day Christ Jesus returns.

So I thank you Father, for believing in me. I know that you are with me. With you is where I belong, and in you I will never thirst or hunger again.

For your word says, "Blessed are those who hunger and thirst after righteousness, for they will be completely satisfied."

So I thank you that I am blessed going in and coming out, in the city and in the field, because you said so, and your word prevails. I pray over those whose tongues rise up against me, because your word says that they shall stumble and fall.

I pray and hope that one day they are saved and set free from the things that contribute to their negative actions, so that they too may live a life of peace and joy.

I lift my hands to you, and I thank you that I am free to be the phenomenal me that you purposed me to be.

Thank you now for your peace that surpasses all understanding. Now unto Him who is able to do exceedingly and abundantly above all I can ask or think, thank you, and it is so done!

Scripture References: GENESIS 1:27, PHILIPPIANS 1:6, 4:7&8, MATTHEW 5:6, 1 JOHN 4:4, ISAIAH 54:17, EXODUS 14:14, EPHESIANS 2:10 & 3:20

Know Your Lines Regarding your Positioning as a Kingdom Citizen

Sometimes as Kingdom Citizens, we tend to forget our positioning. By that I mean, sometimes we forget who we are and how God sees us. Our position is secured by Christ. Our purpose is revealed by God. But when we forget our position, we also forsake our power. How does one lose sight of the position they have as Kingdom Citizens? Quite simple: when we allow certain experiences in our lives to override what our Father has said concerning us. Yes, we will have good days, and yes we will have trying days. Yes we will even have times when we feel overlooked, or times that we feel like God is nowhere to be found. But He said, "I AM always with you! "Who is the "I AM"? He is the Greater One, the one who reigns, the one who can do anything but fail, our strong tower, our waymaker, the one who came, that we might LIVE and Live life more abundantly.

That alone should remind you of who you have in your corner at all times, no matter what it feels like. So, with this in mind, when you have those days where you feel all alone, when you feel like the world is against you, when you feel like all hope is lost, or when you just feel like you are wandering through life, remember your lines!! These lines will steer you and bring you back to your rightful place and positioning, and whether you know it or not, you are one amazing person! You were created to be GREAT!! Even when life situations try and push you down, you can have your little moment, because, yes we are human, but when you are done, remember that your positioning is above and not beneath, so get up, dust yourself off, and speak your lines with boldness and confidence to your God; and watch God renew your strength. Watch His grace abound towards you. Watch His peace transcend your understanding, Watch Him Work on your behalf!

THESE ARE YOUR LINES:

Father I honor you and I thank you for who you are, for it is because of you that I live, move, and have my being.

I have the mind of Christ, and I thank you that as a Believer, my assigned seat is seated at the right hand of the Father in heavenly places.

I thank you that I am a joint heir with Christ, sharing in his spiritual blessings and inheritance, and even in those times where I experience mistreatment, rejection, being overlooked, or just mishandled, I thank you that I am your chosen one, a royal priesthood, a holy nation, and I am more than a conqueror.

I overcome by the blood of the lamb, and I do not conform to the patterns of this world, but I stay in position, by being progressively changed by the renewing of my mind, focusing on Godly values and ethical attitudes, so that I may prove what the will of God is, which is good, acceptable, and perfect.

But Father help me to not think of myself more highly than I should, but to maintain the understanding of my positioning in the kingdom, and my purpose here on earth, which is to bring glory to your name by walking in confidence of who you are in me, and in the measure of faith in which you have given me, to be what you have called me to be.

Now unto Him who is able to do exceedingly and abundantly above all I can ask or think, thank you for helping me understand my positioning, and what you say about me—that is most important, and it is so!

Scripture References: ACTS 17:28, ROMANS 8:37, ROMANS 12:2-4, EPHESIANS 1:20, 2: 4-7, 3:20, 1 PETER 2:9

Know Your Lines In the times of Uncertainty & Worry

I decided to put these two together because they oftentimes come as a couple in our lives. Have you ever prayed about a situation or an issue, and it seemed as if God was not responding fast enough, or moving quick enough? Have you ever been hoping for God to intervene but it seems as if you don't see a thing happen when you want it to? I don't know about you, but typically, the very next day, many of us tend to automatically worry about whether or not God is even listening. Personally, I worry about the what ifs, and I worry about the greatest question of them all—HOW? How will it happen? How will it get paid for? How will I accomplish it in spite of these obstacles?

But in this faith walk, I believe that the uncertain times and moments are a setup for us as believers, because we are either good believers and worship and give thanks to God in the meantime, believing that He will show up and reveal right on time, or we get tired of waiting and make decisions based on our emotions, accompanied by other opinions. This eventually leads us to a place where we need God even more! (All I need is 3 witnesses to attest to this!) Just raise your hand, nobody can see you..lol, but you can see me.. ME! As stated, I believe that these times are moments when we develop the best bond with God, because, we have to have so much confidence in Him, and rely on Him. We have to trust that He loves us, because He loves time with us. He yearns for it. So know that in those times where it feels like everything around you is uncertain, your job is uncertain, your next career move is uncertain, and you may be uncertain about your children's behavior, or you are uncertain about if you will ever be married, or have the right relationships around you; maybe someone reading this is uncertain about how you are going to make it in general with just life circumstances….. but one thing you will know now…. is your lines!! Yes, I know it is easier said than done, especially when you are in the midst of making decisions about the things and people that matter to you most, or when you are just trying to see hope when everything looks unstable, and God seems unreachable. But I come with good news for you!

#1 God is with you.

#2 God is with you.

And #3 The one who knows the plans for your life, and who is the Great I AM, He is with you.

He will NEVER forsake you! Take the believers approach in these times, and speak your lines, while thanking Him at the same time, and I believe he will show up and do His part, and give you the direction, and prompt your spirit and lead you into all truth, and give you wisdom to make the right decisions in your relationships and with your business, and give you the best approach to nurture and lead your children. He can and He will, if you faint not!!

THESE ARE YOUR LINES:

Father, I thank you right where I stand and right where I am, because your word says, "In ALL things, give thanks".

So, in spite of how I feel, I say thank you! Father, you said that if "I acknowledge and trust you in all of my ways, and lean not to my own understanding, that you would direct my path."

So, I take the pressure off of me to know it all, but instead, I will trust that you will help me in this. In addition, you said to, "seek first the kingdom of God and all of His righteousness, and the rest—the answers, the direction—the things will be added."

Father I thank you that you said, "Ask, and keep on asking, and it will be given, seek, and keep on seeking, and I shall find, knock, and keep on knocking and the door will be opened." So I thank you right now Father, that even in this state of uncertainty and worry, I know your word is being activated right now.

Father I rest in knowing that you know the plans for my life, and they are to prosper me, and not to harm me, to give me hope, and an expected end.

Father you told me not to be anxious or worried about anything, but in everything by prayer and petition with thanksgiving, making my specific request known.

So not another moment will I allow the uncertainties and worries that are before me to steal my peace, my joy, or my time, but I come boldly before your throne of grace, understanding that this is a special moment for me and my Father to work together, hand in hand.

So I thank you and I pray and make my request known right now. (Fill in the areas of uncertainty and worry that are applicable, as you pray below, and add if needed, and thank Him for His perfect will being done).

In this area of _____, I need your help. In this area of _____, I need your wisdom. In this area of_____ I need your direction. In this area of_____ I need the best strategy and steps to take. In this area of _____, I need discernment.

And in all areas, I ask your perfect will to be done. Father, you said you wish above all other things, that I would prosper as my soul prospers, so I thank you that I prosper today, and that my soul, my will, and my emotions come subject to the Most High who is able to keep me from falling. Father you also said that if I keep my mind stayed on thee, that you would keep me in your perfect peace, so as I have made my request known in the areas of uncertainty and worry, I turn off worry, the opinions of others, and I bind up anxiety, and I turn my eyes and ears to you, that I may see and hear clearly, and I release all clutter in my mind and I rest in you!

For you also said that if I totally rely and adhere to your word, that I would not be disappointed in your expectations. I choose to believe that your word is working for me right now. Now to Him who is able to do exceedingly and abundantly above all I can ask or think, I thank you that it is so!

Scripture References: ROMANS 10:11, MATTHEW 6:33, 7:7&8, JEREMIAH 29:11, ISAIAH 26:3, PHILIPPIANS 4:6, PROVERBS 3: 5&6

Know your Lines for Protection

For most of us, we have observed a lot of what is going on in the world today, and simply put: it is not pretty. It seems like the bad is outweighing the good, but at the end of the day, as we come to a better understanding of our lines, our positioning, and our purpose, we can and will change the dynamic of this. We must stand together, for our generation, but most importantly, for the now generation, and the generations to come. We as believers must put on the breastplate of righteousness (an upright heart), the helmet of salvation (the sword of the Spirit, which is the word of God), the belt of truth (personal integrity, moral courage), strap your feet with the gospel of peace and preparation, to stand firm-footed, and the shield of faith in order to thrust change in the earth. And get this, not only do we have the backing of heaven, but we have supernatural security, in which all we have to do is say the word, and they are on post and on guard at all times. May I introduce to some, and present to others, our angels. We all have assigned angels, who move at our command, and they are here as our aid to accomplish God's perfect will in our lives. Our Father, God, was so mindful of us that not only did He leave with us, the Holy Spirit, who is our Comforter, our Advocate, our Intercessor, who leads us into all truth, but He also assigned us angels to help us here on earth. What an Awesome, Amazing, Wonderful, Caring, God we serve! In other words, whereever we go, we have everything we need and we have a mighty covering and backing. So rest in this today, and know your lines as it pertains to you as a believer and everything and everyone, connected to you, that the word of truth, has you covered!

THESE ARE YOUR LINES:

Lord, I thank you for being so mindful of me. Not only did you give me the Holy Spirit, but you have assigned angels that are here to assist me and guard me in all of my ways.

Father you said that a thousand may fall at my side, and ten thousand at my right hand, but nothing and no one can touch me.

You said that I will only be a spectator of the things of this world, because you are my refuge, my safe place.

So, I decree and declare Psalm 91 over myself, my family, and everything connected to me, and I thank you Father that we are covered today and everyday.

I also decree and declare Psalm 91 over our youth and millennials in Jesus' Name. I put on the full armor of God today, and I thank you that no weapon formed against us shall prosper, for Greater is He that is in me, than he that is in the world.

Scripture References: PSALM 91, EPHESIANS 6:11-20, JOHN 14:15, JOHN 16:13, ROMANS 8:26; 1 JOHN 4:4

Know Your Lines to
Overcome Fear

As believers, of course we know the scripture that says that "God has not given us a spirit of fear, but He has given us His spirit of power, love, and of sound judgement". So in that, let's deal with that spirit of fear that we as believers wrestle with more than anything else. This specific area of fear that I am speaking about, is the fear of failure. Yes, there are other areas that we wrestle with, but this one seems to be more prominent, because of what life has taught us or brought us, or simply because we have allowed so much negativity and disbelief into our lives to infiltrate our minds, that we don't believe we are capable. We have seemingly lost faith, or we have just stopped believing altogether. And I think it is safe to say, that this fear of failing is one of the reasons why many of us have not tapped fully into our purpose and destiny, or why we have given up on love and meeting new people, or why we haven't aimed higher in our careers, or why going to college or going back to college has only been a thought, just to name a few. But our lines, according to the word of truth, are great reminders of how we can conquer the false advertising that goes on in our mind, and the imaginations that try to magnify itself in certain situations. Our lines remind us of who we have in our corner at all times. He is our Redeemer, He is our Savior, and his name is Jesus. And in His mind, we are well able to do, to be, and to become, everything He has called us to, but we can't give up. We can't allow things to take over our lives, our gifts, our talents, our dreams, our God given abilities. So we say this again, God has not given us a spirit of fear. The spirit of fear is not a part of our benefits package, or our positioning, as believers. So let's overcome this with our lines.

THESE ARE YOUR LINES:

Father I honor you and I acknowledge you today as my light and my salvation, therefore, whom shall I fear.

Father you are the strength of my life of whom shall I be afraid. Father I thank you that you are with me and for me, so therefore who can be successful against me.

Father, today I decree and declare that I am strong and courageous, for the truth is, you are always with me. And you said that when I decree and declare a thing, it shall be established. I appreciate your love towards me, because I understand that your perfect love drives out all fear, and your love never, ever, fails.

So, Father continue to help me to walk in the spirit of power, love, and a sound mind, that I may continue to access and accomplish my goals, dreams, ambitions, and endeavors.

So that I may continue to be the best me for me, and to those around me. I thank you Father that from this day forward, I no longer allow the things that I cannot change, to paralyze me, by staying in fear. But I allow your word to transform me daily, for it is the truth that will make me free. I am more than a conqueror and I have the victory! In Jesus' Name!

Scripture References: PSALM 27:1; ROMANS 8:31 & 37; 1 JOHN 4:18; 2 TIMOTHY 1:7

Know your Lines For Wisdom

So as Kingdom citizens, it is important to understand that we have access to wisdom. What is wisdom? I am so glad that you asked. According to Proverbs 4:7, it says "Wisdom is supreme", and with all your getting, get understanding (actively seek spiritual discernment, mature comprehension, and logical interpretation) AMP bible version. And then verse 8 says, "Prize wisdom, in other words exalt wisdom, and she will exalt you." So to go back and dissect, supreme means high ranking or superior. In other words, wisdom is superior over your thoughts and your ways, because wisdom are thoughts, ideas, and concepts, from God, whose thoughts are higher than ours, and ways are higher than ours. As kingdom citizens, it is important that we invite wisdom into our daily walk, because when we walk with wisdom, verse 12 says "your steps will not be impeded or hindered", and your path will be clear and open. James 1 says "If you lack wisdom, he is to ask, and when you ask, verse 6 says, "you must ask for wisdom in faith, without doubting God's willingness to help you. In other words, trust that he will give you the answer, he will lead you accordingly, he will guide you through the storm, he will provide wise counsel in your marriage, he will help you to discern what company to keep around you and how to make your next career moves, because He is just good and intelligent like that! So if you are ever in the state of confusion, ask for wisdom in faith, for He is not the author of confusion, but Jesus is the Way, the Truth, and the Life! For in Him we live, move, and have our being. So with Wisdom and the Way(Jesus), We Win in the end, for He always causes us to Triumph!

THESE ARE YOUR LINES:

Father I thank you that you are the Way, the Truth, and the Life, and because you are, I have everything I need.

Father I come asking you for wisdom in my _____ (fill in the blank(s).

You said, if I ask for wisdom in faith, believing that you will help me, that you would freely give it to me, so Father I thank you for helping me in this.

I understand that your ways are higher than mine, and your thoughts are too, so I make wisdom supreme and superior over my thoughts, because in the end Father I want your results, and I know that you wish above all things that I would prosper as my soul prospers, and I rest in knowing that you know the plans for my life, so I lean on your wisdom today.

I appreciate your Spirit leading me into all truth, so that I may know how to discern, and better understand how to navigate in this. I honor you and give you praise. Amen!

Scripture References: PROVERBS 4:7, JAMES 1:5&6, JOHN 14:6, ACTS 17:28, 2 CORINTHIANS 2:14, 3 JOHN 1:2, JEREMIAH 29:11

Know Your Lines
For Faith

Initially I started to go into knowing your lines for Healing and Financial needs. And don't get me wrong, these are areas in which we need to know our lines too, because there are times in which we get a doctor's report or seemingly our bills override our income. But something in my spirit said to go straight to faith, because, as believers, this is our standard of living, according to our Father. In addition, when we look in the New Testament, when God began to perform miracles, what was needed to see these miracles, signs, and wonders? You are correct! Faith!!!

So, in this topic, I felt lead to include an all in one approach, because according to Hebrews 11:6, "And without Faith, it is impossible to please God, because anyone who comes to Him must believe that He exists and that he rewards those who earnestly seek Him." In addition, He spoke to us in Heb 10: 38, and said that "My righteous one (the one justified by faith) shall live by faith! And this is just one of the many times, Jesus declared this in the Bible. So let's start with what Faith is, according to our Father.

Hebrews 11:1, says "Faith is the confidence in what we hope for and the assurance about what we do not see. (NIV version). Let's read it in the (AMP bible version). It says, "Now faith (that is with an inherent trust and enduring confidence in the power, wisdom, and goodness of God) is the confirmation of things divinely guaranteed, and the evidence of things not seen." I hope these two translations have broken it down a little more for you, but there are two words that I want to highlight from the Amplified version, and that is **"Enduring Confidence"**. What does this mean to you? To me it sounds like simply put, no matter what, simply believe. So even when things seemingly feel like they are against you, with enduring confidence, see it with your spiritual eye first.

I know this can be a challenge initially, trust me, I know. But we have to practice it, because our truth is that we are Spirit, and we live in an earthly suit (our body), and we possess a soul. But at first glance, we have to see by faith, that even this is working together for our good. At first glance we should see it as being an opportunity for God to remove, restore, redo, remodel, recover, heal, and set free. After all, "He knows the plans, and He has factored in all of our ups and downs, mistakes and trials, and His plans are always to prosper and not harm.

If you should find yourself in need financially, by faith, understand that He is your shepherd and you shall not want for anything (Psalm 23:1). By faith, bring the tithes and offerings into the storehouse, and see if He will not pour out a blessing you will not have room enough to receive, and He will rebuke the devourer for your sake, AND, All nations shall call you happy and blessed, for you shall be a land of delight." (Malachi 3:10-12)

I can remember a time when I was unemployed for two years, and received an unemployment check, I would give my tithes and offerings from that, and I saw the hand of the Lord working every time. Why? Because I moved by Faith (Enduring Confidence in his power, wisdom, and goodness). So right here in this moment, in addition to saying "know your lines", I also want to say, "know your MOVE!" Faith without works is useless! Our Father is a God of order, and as we move with wisdom (spiritual insight), and by Faith (Enduring confidence in the power, wisdom, and goodness of God) I believe God will make His move, because at that moment, there is <u>ACTION REQUIRED</u>!

The same with believing God for healing, and to connect you with healthy relationships. By faith, believe that You are healed by His stripes, but also activate and awaken that champion in you.

Take the necessary steps to be and become stronger and healthier. It's your Move! It is not over until God says it is over. But it is automatically over if you faint, if you give up. Wake up Champion! Believe in His Power again and believe that He created you to do good works in the earth!

And switching gears, to my single ladies and those of you who are waiting on the right relationships and the right connections for your business ventures and endeavors. By faith, believe that according to Ecclesiastes 3:11, God makes everything beautiful in His timing. By faith, believe that as you seek Him and after Him, and ask for his advice and wisdom, He will add these things, and show you who is who, and what business partnerships are right for you. So your move (works) is doing the research, asking for the spirit of discernment as you are scheduling the meeting or if you are stepping out and meeting someone new, and actually listening to that which gives you peace.

In conclusion, I know I did this subject a little differently, but this is what my spirit was led to do, because in the grand scheme of things, this is our mode of operation and currency in the Kingdom of God.

So instead of a prayer here, I would like to admonish you to read and meditate on this and the scripture references below. I believe as you do, you will begin to see things from a God perspective, you will begin to see God results in areas of your life, and you will begin to taste and see that the Lord is Good…. All the Time!

Scripture References: HEBREWS 11:1&6, HEBREWS 10:38, MALACHI 3:10-12, PSALM 23:1, ISAIAH 53:5, ECCLESIASTES 3:11

Know Your Lines for Love

In the beginning of this book, I related my title to a play or a movie. And with every good play or movie, there is always a "Big Finish" or the part that brings it all together. Sometimes, it's a happy ending, sometimes it's a sad ending, but because God is a God of Love, this is going to be LOVE ending!

I know most of you are probably going to go ahead and close the book up on this one...lol

However, one of the greatest commandments, as Kingdom citizens, is to Love God with all of our heart, mind, and spirit. And then...drumroll please... He commanded us to Love our neighbors, as we love ourselves. But wait! That's not all!! He said, you can have all of the faith in the world, but if you do not have love, it is null and void! We cannot let the world outdo us and put so much fear in us, that we forget to display the greatest commandment! Now listen my brothers and sisters, I know that this is not always easy to do with most people, and these days, you still have to use wisdom as it pertains to how to represent the love of Christ, because people can and sometimes will take advantage. So with that being said, choose love in spite of, and also ask God for wisdom on how to approach and follow through. I hope that makes sense to you.

The truth of the matter is, there is no greater love than a man who would lay down HIS life for us. God gave His only son Jesus, so that we could live and not just live any kind of way, but live life abundantly. He did this, for you and me! He made the ultimate sacrifice. That's Love!

So metaphorically, sometimes we have to lay our feelings aside, or our emotions aside, for the sake of sharing the love of Jesus, and yes, sometimes, that is an Ultimate Sacrifice!..lol Let's just be real about it. But here is something to ponder, what if you choose to do something that saves someone, heals someone from a broken past, gives someone hope that day, that they didn't have, wouldn't you say that it was worth it? The power and the Love of God saves, heals, and sets the captives free. And God is counting on us to do our best in this. But don't beat yourself up if you don't always get it right, because His love is the only love that is perfect and unconditional. By doing our best and asking for wisdom, I believe that is all that He requires. So let's guard our hearts, but do our best to intentionally love those around us, for the simple fact that it pleases our Father, and that should be our hearts desire.

On a side note, while I was typing this, this thought came to me. So God asked us to love our neighbors as ourselves... But the thought that came to mind was, what if we don't love ourselves? What if we have been through so many situations and failed relationships, that we are unsure of how to love, or what it looks like, because we haven't seen a good representation of it, and so with that being said, it is even more difficult to show it, if you don't know it. Well for those of you who need this, let me introduce you to our Father God. In the book of Genesis, when God created mankind, He took His time with us, he did not rush. He was intentional with everything he placed in us and He said "It is Good". And not only that, God said that He created us in His image. So to bring this home, God is so many great things, but two things in particular I would like to point out is that, He is perfect in all of His ways, and so is His love. He gave His only son Jesus, to sacrifice His life for us, not just to live and have a regular life, but have life more abundantly. Understand that true love GIVES, and it doesn't take away so much of you, and the "good" in you, that you are no longer who God created you to be. So if you can get this understanding first, and assess your life experiences/lessons, and/or relationships, and understand whether they were good, challenging, or indifferent, they are all still working together for your good, I believe you will begin to see that not only are you worth being loved, but when you experience this Love (Jesus), you will know how to more effectively love one another.

Does this mean you have to befriend everyone you come in contact with, or give all of you to everyone? Not exactly. This just means being a little more compassionate about those around you and discerning how to show the Love of God to others. I believe in you, and I believe you can do it. Embrace the Love of Jesus today. He loves you more than you know, and He wish above all other things that you would prosper, and be in health, even as your soul (your mind, will, and emotions) prospers. So again, I present to some, and introduce to others, Jesus! He is the best representation of Love that you will ever meet. I have searched all over, and I couldn't find another like Him. I pray that you embrace His love, and that there is a new day dawning for you to love again, as this the heart of our God.

Scripture References: I CORINTHIANS 13:13, MATTHEW 22:37-39; JOHN 3:16, JOHN 10: 10, ROMANS 8: 28, PSALM 18:30, PSALM 145: 8,17; 3 JOHN 1: 2, MATTHEW 5: 7&8, 13-16 (MSG)

The Conclusion of the Whole Matter

I believe the benefits of knowing our lines as kingdom citizens, especially in these times, can be summed up with the following:

1. *So that we can begin to see God results (miracles, signs, wonders)*

2. *So that we can continue to be the "Salt" in the earth, so that others can see God*

3. *So we will no longer question "who we are" and "why we are here"*

Many of us are still trying to understand who and whose we are. We have learned according to the word, that Jesus is the vine and we are the branches, and apart from the vine, we bear no fruit. We only see what we see. We stay stagnate and I believe stagnation strips us little by little of the truth that lies within us. (John 15:5)

We allow the world to place labels and identify us and our worth. When the truth of the matter is, God gave us as Kingdom citizens, as born again believers, charge over the earth! He said rule and he commanded us to be fruitful and multiply! He even said, that whoever believes in me will do the works that I have been doing, and……. YOU will do even greater, because He is! (John 14:12) Hear ye my sisters and brothers, when you grasp that alone, I believe you will see yourself the way He sees you more and more each day!

In conclusion, it is time out for just living and going through the motions! I am asking God to REVIVE US again! It is time to LIVE and see God's results in our lives! But it only works, when we work the word of Truth!

I pray that this will be a resource that will always be a blessing to you! Now go and Be Fruitful and allow God to Shine through you! #KnowYourLines